THE YOUNG
OXFORD
LIBRARY OF
SCIENCE

Energy and Forces

Neil Ardley

OXFORD
UNIVERSITY PRESS

OXFORD
UNIVERSITY PRESS

Great Clarendon Street, Oxford OX2 6DP

Oxford University Press is a department of the University of Oxford.
It furthers the University's objective of excellence in research, scholarship,
and education by publishing worldwide in

Oxford New York

Auckland Bangkok Buenos Aires Cape Town Chennai
Dar es Salaam Delhi Hong Kong Istanbul Karachi
Kolkata Kuala Lumpur Madrid Melbourne Mexico City Mumbai
Nairobi São Paulo Shanghai Singapore Taipei Tokyo Toronto

Oxford is a registered trade mark of Oxford University Press
in the UK and in certain other countries

British Library Cataloguing in Publication Data available

Hardback ISBN 0-19-910948-6
Paperback ISBN 0-19-910949-4

1 3 5 7 9 10 8 6 4 2

Designed and typeset by Full Steam Ahead
Printed in Malaysia.

CONTENTS

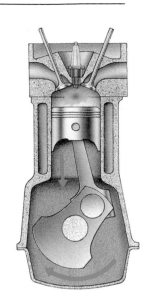

MAKING IT HAPPEN

Do you have days when you want to run, jump, shout, sing and be very active? If you do, people will say that you are 'bursting with energy', and they would be right. You need energy to do these things, and all the other actions that you carry out every day.

Every action of any kind needs energy to make it happen – not just here on Earth but throughout the entire Universe. Energy makes your body work so that you can see, hear, think, speak, move and do all kinds of things. Energy keeps all living things – including us – alive. This energy comes from the Sun's heat and from food.

But non-living things use energy too. All machines need a supply of energy to work, and they stop when their energy supply gives out or is turned off. Machines get energy from fuels, such as petrol, or from a supply of power such as electricity or running water.

FROM CORNFLAKES TO CONSERVATION

Many foods have their energy value printed on the packet. It is in kilojoules (kJ), or thousands of joules. A joule is a unit that scientists use to measure energy. It is named after the British scientist James Prescott Joule (1818–1889). He discovered the principle of conservation of energy in the 1840s, which says that energy cannot be destroyed, but changes its form.

What is energy?

Energy makes things happen, and it takes several different forms. The energy in movement is just one of them. Other forms of energy include light and sound, which you use to see and hear things, and heat, which keeps you warm.

Your body has a large amount of stored energy, which keeps it working. Non-living things may contain stored energy too. A battery is a store of electricity, which is yet another form of energy.

◄ Petrol stores a lot of energy. As it burns in this dragster's engine, the petrol's chemical energy changes to heat energy. This heat energy changes to kinetic (movement) energy as the engine drives the car along.

key words
- action
- joule
- kinetic energy
- potential energy

▼ Most of our energy comes through space from the Sun in the form of heat and light. After arriving on Earth, the energy may change its form several times as it is used. Every set of changes ends with the production of heat or light.

Plants use light energy from the Sun to grow. The light energy becomes chemical energy and is stored inside the plant.

All animals (including us) get their food from plants – or from eating other animals that have eaten plants.

The Sun powers the world's weather systems – even when it is not a sunny day! Heat energy makes winds blow and water evaporate into the air to form rain clouds.

Wind turbines harness the power of the wind and turn their kinetic energy into electricity that will power machines.

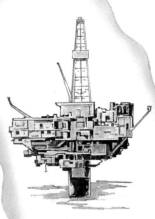

Rigs drill for oil on the seabed. Oil is an important source of fuel. It is formed from the remains of living things.

Fuels such as oil and coal are burned in power stations. The chemical energy inside the fuels is turned into electrical energy.

The chemical energy in food allows people and animals to move and play. Their bodies change the chemical energy into kinetic (movement) energy.

Electrical energy powers machines, such as high-speed trains. It changes into kinetic energy as the motor turns and drives the train along the track.

Using energy

Energy is needed for an action of any kind to happen. This energy has to come from somewhere. You get energy from food and drink. An electrical machine, such as a radio, gets a supply of electrical energy (electricity) from a power point or a battery.

Although every action needs some energy to happen, it does not use up the energy. Energy cannot be destroyed. Instead, it changes form as the action happens. For example, when you throw a ball, the muscles in your arm take some of your stored energy, which has come from food, and change it into energy of movement. A computer takes electrical energy from a power point and changes it into light energy as a picture appears on the screen.

You need about 10,000 kilojoules of energy every day to keep your body working. Most of this energy comes from your food, and it is about the same amount of energy as there is in a 500-gram box of cereal.

The source of our energy

Our main supplies of energy are food to make our bodies work and fuels to drive our machines. We eat plants, or meat and fish which come from animals that ate plants. So all the energy in our food comes from plants. Our main fuels are coal, oil and gas. All these fuels are the remains of animals and plants that lived millions of years ago. So the energy in fuel comes from plants, too.

But plants are not the original source of this energy. They are just energy stores. The energy that they store comes from the Sun. As plants grow, they turn the Sun's light and heat into stored energy. In fact, the source of almost all the energy on Earth is the rays of heat and light that stream through space from the Sun.

▼ Strip lights use less energy than most light bulbs, which get warm and change much of the electricity they use into heat energy instead of light.

▶ When a jack-in-the-box jumps out at you, it changes energy stored in its spring into energy of movement. The stored energy is also called potential energy.

ENERGY ON THE MOVE

To a radio wave, your body is like glass! Just as light comes through a window, radio waves and other kinds of wave or ray are streaming through your body right now. You cannot feel them and they cause you no harm, but they bring radio and television programmes to your home.

Radio and television sets receive radio waves sent out from high masts or satellites. The waves carry sounds and pictures to all sets within range, passing through walls and people on the way.

Radio waves are electromagnetic waves, a group of penetrating waves. Some of these waves are also called rays. Other kinds of penetrating waves and rays include microwaves, which carry mobile telephone calls, heat rays, which bring you warmth, and light rays, which let you see everything around you.

Sound waves are different kinds of waves that can pass through air and solid materials. They let you hear all kinds of sounds and noises, such as people talking or music playing.

Bringing energy to all

All rays and waves transport energy from one place to another. They spread out from their source in all directions, and bring their energy to everything that they meet.

When you speak, your mouth sends out sound waves. These spread out through the air, and perhaps through thin walls, carrying sound energy. When the sound waves enter the ears of other people, they hear you.

In the same way, rays spread out through space from the Sun. They carry heat energy and light energy to the Earth, giving us warmth and daylight.

Making waves

Water waves, from ripples in a pond to giant breakers at the seashore, also

BRIGHT SPARK

The German scientist Heinrich Hertz (1857–1894) discovered radio waves in 1888. He did this by using a powerful electric current to make a spark, and saw that another spark immediately jumped across a gap in a brass ring nearby. The first spark produced radio waves that travelled through the air to the ring. The waves produced an electric current in the ring, causing the second spark. Radio communications were invented as a result of Hertz's discovery.

▲ A good surfer can ride a giant wave for a long way. The surfer is able to stay at the front of the wave and move along with it.

transport energy. If you drop a stone into a pond, the water moves up and down as the stone enters the water. This up-and-down movement, or vibration, travels out across the water surface as a wave. When it meets a floating object such as a toy boat, the wave makes it bob up and down. The energy to make the boat bob comes from the falling stone, and is carried out to the boat by the wave.

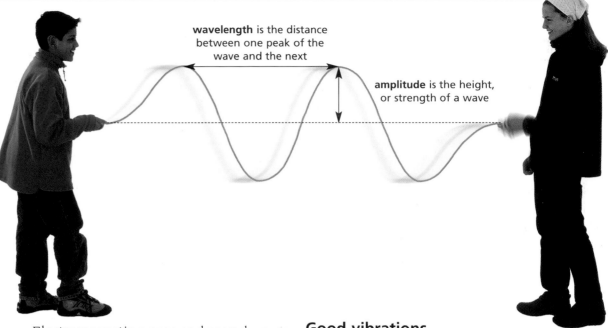

▶ Demonstrate a wave. Tie a rope to a tree or get a friend to hold one end. Hold the other end fairly tightly and move it quickly up and down. A wave travels along the rope. As the wave passes, the rope goes up and down or vibrates at a particular rate. This is called the frequency of the wave.

wavelength is the distance between one peak of the wave and the next

amplitude is the height, or strength of a wave

Light rays, like all electromagnetic waves, move at 300,000 kilometres per second. Sound waves travel a million times slower.

Electromagnetic waves and sound waves transport energy as vibrations just as water waves do, which is why they are called 'waves' or 'wave motions'. Heat rays and light rays are wave motions too, and are sometimes called waves instead of rays.

Every kind of wave has a particular frequency, or rate at which it vibrates. A high-frequency wave vibrates quickly, while lower-frequency waves vibrate more slowly.

Good vibrations

Objects can vibrate in a similar way to water waves. When you twang a stretched rubber band, it moves rapidly to and fro. A swing and a pendulum are other examples of vibration. When objects vibrate, they move to and fro at a regular rate. That is why pendulums and vibrating springs and crystals can be used to control clocks and watches and make sure they keep time.

● key words

- frequency
- ray
- vibration
- wave
- wave motion

▶ Strong winds can cause structures to vibrate slowly. In 1940, the Tacoma Narrows Bridge in the United States collapsed because the wind made it vibrate more and more. Bridges like this are now strengthened so that vibration does not build up.

PUSH AND PULL

W hat lifts a plane from the ground and sends it zooming through the air? An engine moves the plane forwards, and more forces operate under the wings, holding the plane up. Forces are at work everywhere all the time. Many are powerful enough to crush you, others so weak that you cannot feel them.

A force is a push or a pull. You exert a force when you kick a ball or open a book. When anything begins to move, a force starts it off. Forces also make moving things speed up, slow down, stop or change direction. You use a pulling force to stop a lively dog on a lead.

But forces do not disappear when things are not moving. All the parts of a building – the floors, walls and beams – push or pull on each other. These forces exactly balance. If they didn't, a part of the building would begin to move and the whole structure might collapse.

▶ Strong internal forces between the particles inside a pole-vaulter's pole give it elasticity and stop it from breaking. Instead, the pole bends, then springs back to thrust the vaulter into the air.

FORCES

All the forces that make things move or hold things together are composed of a few basic forces. Electrostatic force, magnetic force and the force of gravity are three of these basic forces.

Rubbing a balloon makes it stick to a wall with **electrostatic force.**

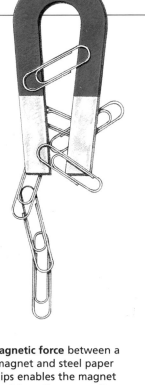

Magnetic force between a magnet and steel paper clips enables the magnet to pick up the paper clips.

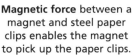

Gravity is the force that makes things fall to the ground when you drop them.

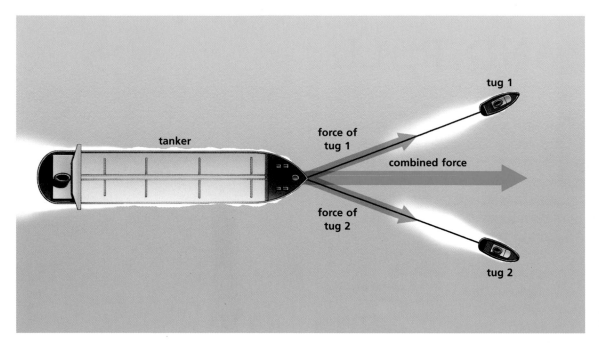

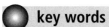

◀ If several forces act on an object, they combine to create one overall force. Here, the forces from the two tugs combine to produce a force that pulls the tanker forwards.

key words
• atoms
• springs
• weight

Sources of forces

In people and animals, muscles produce the force to move arms, legs and other body parts. Machines have motors or engines to produce force. Magnets attract other magnets, exerting force that is put to use in electric motors. Springs drive machines such as wind-up clocks or toy mice. When you wind them up, the spring inside stretches and then it contracts to produce a force. This makes the clock hands move round or the mouse shoot across the floor.

Another force – gravity – is present everywhere in the Universe. It makes things fall or roll down slopes. Gravity also makes everything press down on the ground with a force, and this force is their weight.

Adapting or breaking

What happens when forces try to move fixed objects? The objects adapt by changing shape. They may get smaller or bigger, bend, twist or even snap! When you pull a rubber band, you can see it stretch. But many things change shape so little that you cannot see it happening.

▶ On a rollercoaster ride at a theme park the carriages are first raised to a great height, and then released. The force of gravity gives them enough power to complete the ride, even when they loop the loop.

Inside forces

Everything that exists is made up of tiny particles called atoms, or groups of atoms called molecules. Forces between the particles cause them to grip each other and hold things together. These internal forces are strong in hard, tough materials such as steel. But they are weak in liquids and gases, such as air and water. Because the internal forces in liquids and gases are weak, the particles can move about more, and the materials can flow easily.

GETTING GOING

Kick a ball. You can feel the force that you use to start it soaring through the air. But why does the ball keep moving through the air? This puzzled people for centuries, for the answer seems unbelievable. The answer is that nothing keeps it moving – it goes by itself.

To get anything moving, a force must push on it or pull on it. But once something is already moving, like a ball soaring or rolling, it does not need a force to continue moving. It carries on of its own accord, moving effortlessly in the same direction and at a constant speed. You continue to move unaided when you slide on some ice or roll along on skates...until you hit a wall!

Speed, turn, slow or stop

Once an object is moving, it will not speed up (accelerate), slow down or change direction unless another force acts on it. This happens all the time. A soaring ball is slowed by the air, which exerts a backward force called friction as the ball moves through it. The ball also slows down and soon stops rising because the force of gravity pulls it down. At the same time, the force of a gust of wind may blow the ball to one side and change its direction.

If a force pushes or pulls on one side or one end of an object, or if two forces act on both sides or both ends, then the object turns. You grip the ends of the handlebars of a bicycle to turn them.

More weight, less speed

Have you ever tried to push a car to get it moving? Even though the car can roll easily, it needs several people to push it and takes a lot of force to get it going. This is because the car is very heavy. The more you all push, the faster it goes. Slowing and stopping a heavy object needs a lot of force too, so a car has powerful brakes.

key words
- accelerate
- brakes
- motion
- speed

▶ When skydivers leap from an aircraft, they accelerate as gravity pulls them towards the ground. But the faster they fall, the greater the friction of the air around them. Eventually the forces of air friction and gravity balance out and the skydiver falls at a constant speed of about 200 kilometres per hour.

Pushing back and moving forwards

How do you jump? You push down on the ground with your legs. But surely, to move upwards, you need a force that pushes you up? Where does that force come from? It comes from the ground, which pushes you up as you push down on it. Forces always act in pairs like this.

Out of this world

Movement is different in space. The Earth, stars, planets and moons were moving as they formed and cannot stop. Space is empty, and there is no air to produce friction and stop them. In the same way, spacecraft and satellites enter space at high speed and, if they do not return to Earth, will continue to move for ever.

You are never at rest. The Earth moves through space, circling the Sun at a speed of 108,000 kilometres per hour, and carrying you along with it.

▼ As the water spurts from a high-power hose, it pushes back on the nozzle. It takes a lot of strength for the firefighters to hold the nozzle steady and stop it pushing them back.

▼ A ride on a bicycle involves several different forces as you start off, speed up, turn, slow down and stop.

You push off and pedal to start moving.
The force of your legs goes to the back wheel, which turns and moves the bicycle forwards. The bicycle speeds up.

You reach a steady speed on the flat.
A backward force called friction comes into action as the bicycle moves. It equals the forward force on the back wheel. There is no overall force so the bicycle's speed is constant.

Travelling downhill, the force of gravity pulls you forwards, and you do not need to pedal.

Travelling uphill, gravity pulls you backwards. You have to pedal hard to produce enough forward force to overcome gravity.

You swivel the handlebars to turn the bicycle. A sideways force moves the front wheel to the side and you change direction.

You apply the brakes.
The brakes produce a backward force on both wheels of the bicycle, and you slow down and stop.

GRINDING TO A HALT

You pedal hard to get a bicycle up to speed. And yet to stop, all you do is grip the brake levers lightly. How can just a gentle pull of the hands so quickly cancel out all the power you put into pedalling? Friction comes to your aid.

As you brake, blocks in the brakes rub against the rim of each wheel. Tiny irregularities in the surfaces of the brake blocks and the rim catch on each other. This produces a strong force, called friction, that acts to slow and stop the wheel rim.

Friction occurs whenever two objects meet, or when an object comes into contact with a liquid such as water, or a gas such as air. If they are moving, then friction slows or stops them. If they are still but try to move, it may prevent movement from starting.

Using friction

Brakes are just one use of friction. It is also needed for a vehicle to move in the first place. Friction enables the wheels to grip the ground so that they do not slide.

 key words

- atoms
- lubrication
- molecules

▶ Cars have powerful disc brakes. A pair of brake pads close and grip a disc attached to the wheel hub, producing a powerful force of friction between the pads and the disc.

All the many things that are held together by screws or nuts and bolts would fall apart without friction. Friction gives the screw a strong grip on the wood around it, or a nut on the metal bolt.

Reducing friction

Friction is not always useful. In moving parts it produces heat, which could damage machines. Oil or grease is used to make the moving parts slippery. This is called lubrication and it reduces friction and heat. This is why you oil the chain on your bicycle.

Lubrication makes a surface smooth because the oil or grease smoothes out any irregularities in the surface. A smooth surface has little friction. Ice is very smooth, which is why you slip on it.

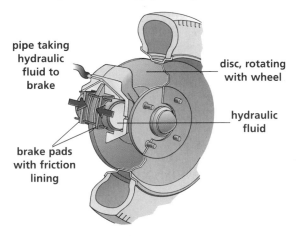

pipe taking hydraulic fluid to brake

disc, rotating with wheel

hydraulic fluid

brake pads with friction lining

◀ The undersides of skis are very smooth so that there is very little friction between the skis and the snow, enabling the skier to move very fast. However, friction comes into play as the skier tilts the skis to grip the snow and change direction.

MAKING LIGHT WORK

Imagine being hungry and thirsty, and having only canned food and drinks in corked bottles – but no can opener or corkscrew to open them. You would have to use your bare hands – a difficult and dangerous business! Every day, tools make all sorts of tasks possible.

▶ Nutcrackers are a kind of lever. The hand is much further from the hinge than the nut, and this magnifies the effort of the hand so that it becomes strong enough to crack the nut.

All sorts of tools, such as can-openers, corkscrews, hammers and spanners, are operated by hand. They work by increasing the amount of force you can exert with your hands or fingers. These devices are simple machines.

Powered machines, such as cars and excavators, have engines and motors to produce force. But they may also contain simple machines, such as levers and gears, to increase the amount of force driving the wheels, buckets or other parts.

Greater effort required

Every machine needs a force to drive it, and this driving force is called the effort. The machine magnifies the effort and applies it to a load, which may move.

You can lift the side of a car using a jack. The effort is the light force of your hand turning the jack handle, while the load is the great weight of the car. The jack greatly increases the force of your hand until it is equal to the weight of the car and raises it.

key words
- effort
- gear
- lever
- load
- weight

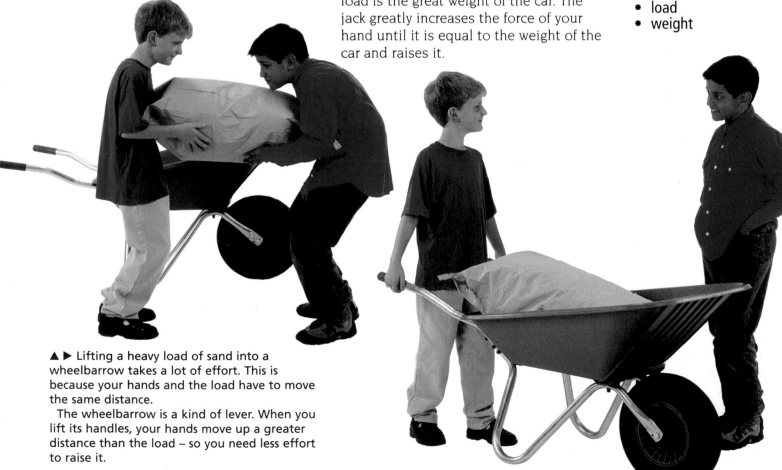

▲ ▶ Lifting a heavy load of sand into a wheelbarrow takes a lot of effort. This is because your hands and the load have to move the same distance.

The wheelbarrow is a kind of lever. When you lift its handles, your hands move up a greater distance than the load – so you need less effort to raise it.

LEVERS

You can use a lever to raise a heavy load, using an effort equal to only half the load, if the effort is twice as far from the pivot as the load. But the load moves only half as far as the end of the lever where the effort is being applied.

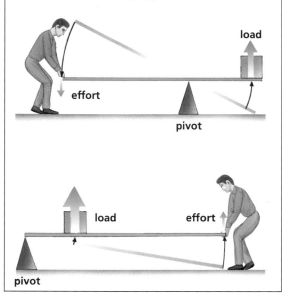

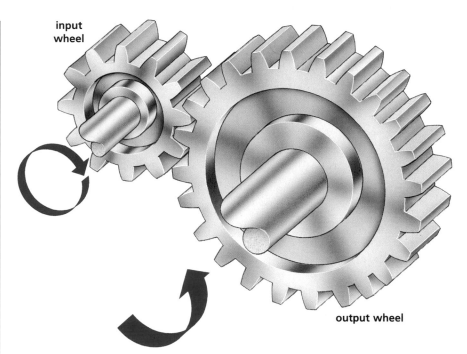

▲ Principles of gearwheels: the small gearwheel turns the larger gearwheel more slowly, but with more force in the opposite direction.

The jack works because you have to turn the handle many times to raise the car's wheel just off the ground. Your hand travels a greater distance than the car rises. Simple machines trade force and distance like this. By moving a greater distance than the load, the light effort is magnified to match the heavy load.

Levers and gears

The most common kinds of simple machines are levers and gears. Levers are rods or bars used to move things. You push one end to exert a force at the other end of the lever or another part of it. Pliers, nutcrackers and bottle openers are levers, and pianos, bicycle brakes and excavators use levers. Spanners and screwdrivers are levers that move in a circle.

Car and bicycle gears contain toothed wheels that mesh together or are connected by a chain. The gearwheels are different sizes and rotate at different speeds, so that they can increase or decrease the force. You can ride up a hill in low gear on a bicycle because you pedal more quickly and this increases the force that turns the back wheel.

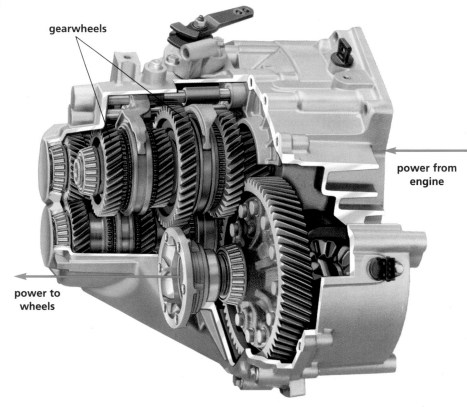

▲ The gearbox in a car connects a shaft from the engine to a shaft that turns the wheels. Changing gear makes different gearwheels connect the shafts so that the engine can turn the car's wheels at different speeds and with different amounts of force.

PUTTING ON THE SQUEEZE

Try to stop the water gushing from a tap by covering the spout – and you will probably end up soaked! That is because the flow of water is too strong to stop.

The water in the tap has a high pressure. It pushes against the inside of the tap with a large amount of force. Water comes out with great force when the tap is turned on.

DOWN DEEP

In 1960, two people descended 11 kilometres to the deepest part of the ocean in an underwater craft called *Trieste*. The pressure of the water there was equal to a weight of just over a tonne on every square centimetre of the cabin (a square centimetre is about the same size as a thumbnail). The cabin had to be very strong to resist this enormous pressure.

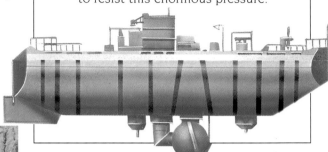

Using pressure

Bicycles, cars and other road vehicles all run on air! The high pressure of the air in the tyres holds the wheel rims above the road surface. Pumps inflate tyres by raising air pressure so that air flows through the valve into the tyre. The valve stops the high-pressure air from escaping.

◀ An excavator works by hydraulics. A pump raises the pressure of hydraulic fluid and sends the fluid through hoses to moving parts such as the bucket, which it drives with great power. The driver controls the fluid's movement to make the bucket scoop up dirt.

Raising pressure

The pressure in a tap is high because the pipe leading to the tap goes back to a tank above it. The weight of all the water in the pipe and tank gives it pressure. If the tank is not higher than the tap, a pump may raise the pressure of the water.

Gases, such as air, also have a certain pressure just as water does. The weight of all the air above you presses in on your body. When you breathe in, the pressure of the surrounding air makes it flow into your lungs.

Solid things exert pressure too. Your weight makes your feet press down on the ground with a certain amount of pressure.

▶ When you suck through a straw, you expand your lungs to lower the air pressure inside them. The outside air pressing on the drink is at a greater pressure, and forces the drink up the straw into your mouth.

air presses down on drink

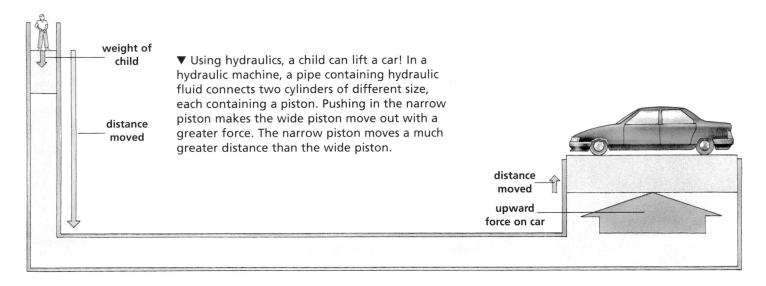

▼ Using hydraulics, a child can lift a car! In a hydraulic machine, a pipe containing hydraulic fluid connects two cylinders of different size, each containing a piston. Pushing in the narrow piston makes the wide piston move out with a greater force. The narrow piston moves a much greater distance than the wide piston.

weight of child

distance moved

distance moved

upward force on car

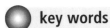

key words

- hydraulic
- pneumatic
- pump
- valve
- weight

Pumps raise the pressure of water in fountains to make the water spurt upwards. Pneumatic machines, such as road-mending drills, use air pressure, while hydraulic machines, such as car brakes and diggers, use liquid pressure. For both types of machine, pumps produce high-pressure air or liquid to drive the moving parts.

No pressure

Pumps can also remove air from a container to reduce the pressure inside. There is a vacuum in the container when the air has gone. The walls of a vacuum flask contain a vacuum, which keeps food or drink inside the flask hot or cold for several hours.

▶ A diver carries a cylinder of compressed (squashed) air in order to breathe underwater. This limits the time of the dive – it is not safe to breathe high-pressure air for very long.

ON AND UNDER THE WATER

Push an empty plastic bottle with a cap into a bowl of water. Push hard, as the water pushes back strongly. Let go, and the bottle springs back up and floats. It is this force in water that makes things float.

As the bottle enters the water, it pushes aside or displaces water. The weight of this displaced water pushes back on the bottle, forcing it upwards. This upward force overcomes the weight of the bottle and the bottle rises until it floats.

All things that float, such as pieces of wood or hollow objects, get enough upward force from the displaced water to equal their weight.

To sink, or not to sink

If the weight of an object is always more than the upward force of the displaced water, then it sinks. This is why heavy stones and bricks sink.

◀ The ancient Greek scientist Archimedes once got into a full bath and made it overflow. He realized that immersing an object provided a simple way of measuring its volume. Archimedes' discovery led him to explain why things float.

▶ Even non-swimmers cannot sink in the Dead Sea. The water there is so salty that it gives more upward force than fresh water or ordinary seawater.

key words
- displacement
- float
- force
- weight

Solid pieces of metal sink too, but not hollow metal objects such as ships and boats. Submarines and submersibles vary their weight to float, dive and return to the surface.

SUBMARINES
Submarines are ocean-going vessels that can travel on the surface or underwater. Submersibles are smaller vessels, some of which are remote-controlled. Both submarines and submersibles have ballast tanks which can be filled with air or water. To dive underwater, the tanks are filled with water to make the vessel heavier. To return to the surface, water is blown out of the ballast tanks by compressed air. This makes the vessel lighter, and it rises again.

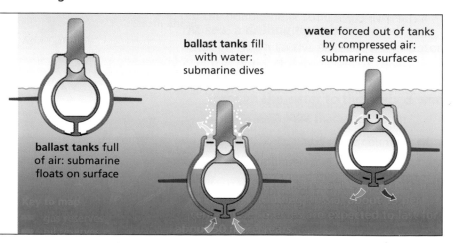

ballast tanks fill with water: submarine dives

water forced out of tanks by compressed air: submarine surfaces

ballast tanks full of air: submarine floats on surface

UP IN THE AIR

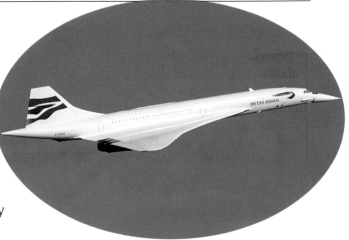

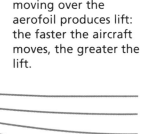

A jumbo jet is like 100 cars all in the air at once – it transports about the same number of people and weighs about the same too. How does such a heavy machine stay up? It all depends on how the air flows around it.

Aircraft of all kinds and flying animals such as birds or butterflies can fly because they have wings. As the wing cuts through the air, air flowing around it creates a force called lift which pushes the wing upwards. It supports the wing (and everything attached to it) in the air.

Helicopters have wings too. As the whirling blades of the helicopter's rotor cut through the air, they work like moving wings to create lift.

▼ Aircraft wings give an arched cross-section called an aerofoil. Air moving over the aerofoil produces lift: the faster the aircraft moves, the greater the lift.

wing   air flow

▼ A glider has no engine, so it is towed along the ground to get up enough speed to take off. Once in the air, it flies at a slight downward angle to keep up enough speed for the wings to generate lift. To regain height, the pilot may fly to a rising air current and circle in it.

▲ Concorde is the fastest airliner ever to have flown. It flies at twice the speed of sound (about 2000 kilometres per hour), more than twice as fast as other airliners.

How wings work

When you fly a kite, the wind hits its underside and pushes the kite upwards. A wing works partly like a kite. It slopes at an angle so that its underside hits the air. Air is pushed out of its way and the air forces the wing upwards.

Wings also get lift from the way the air flows over them. The top of the wing is curved, so the air moves rapidly up and over. When air moves faster, its pressure drops. The air under the wing has a higher pressure because it moves more slowly, and this higher pressure also forces the wing upwards.

Up into the air ... and down again

To take off in the first place, aircraft speed along a runway until they are going so fast that the lift overcomes their weight and they fly. Birds can flap their wings to produce lift to take off from the ground, or simply open their wings and jump off a perch. Helicopters whirl their rotors until the blades generate enough lift, and then they go straight up.

When an aircraft, helicopter or bird is flying level, its lift equals its weight.

 key words

- flow
- lift
- streamlining
- weight
- wing

▲ A bird flaps its wings to generate lift, the upward force that holds it in the air, and to propel itself forwards. Once the bird is moving, it may hold its wings out straight and soar, getting lift from the way the air flows around its wings.

Slowing, or altering the rotors, decreases the lift, and it begins to descend and may land.

Flow and friction

When anything moves through air, the air parts and flows around it. The air rubs against the moving object's surface, producing a force called friction that slows its speed. The same thing happens when an object moves through water. Reducing friction helps to gain speed, and saves fuel.

One way to achieve this is by a streamlined design. Streamlined shapes are narrow and dart-like. A pointed nose or bow makes it easier to cut through the air or water. A smooth surface or skin allows the air or water to rub as little as possible. Streamlining is important for aircraft, cars and ships, and for animals such as fish and birds.

As an airliner takes off and lands, flaps come out from the back of the wings. These flaps are like extra wings. They enable the wings to generate more lift at slow speeds.

◄ The design of an aircraft, such as this jet fighter, can be checked out in a wind tunnel. Air is blown over a model at high speed. The designer studies how the air flows around the model plane, to see how the real aircraft will behave when it flies through the air.

ALL PULL TOGETHER

However hard you toss a ball up into the air, it will fall back down. A mysterious force called gravity pulls everything towards the ground. It's mysterious because no one knows why gravity exists – it's one of the great unsolved questions of science.

Gravity pulls whole objects together. If they are free to move, then gravity gets them moving. This is why raindrops, autumn leaves and balls fall towards the ground, the surface of our planet Earth.

key words
- field
- force
- mass
- weight

Forces and fields

Whenever two objects are near each other, gravity acts between them and tries to pull them together. The strength of the force depends on the mass (the amount of material) in both objects. Because our planet is so massive, there is a strong force of gravity between the Earth and everything that is on or near it.

The Earth's field of gravity extends out into space to the Moon and beyond. Gravity keeps the Moon in its orbit or path around the Earth. In the same way, the Sun's gravity holds the Earth, and all the other planets of the Solar System, in their orbits around the Sun.

FROM AN APPLE TO THE UNIVERSE

As a young man, British scientist Isaac Newton (1642–1727) saw an apple fall from a tree. Of course, he wasn't the first to see this, but he was the first to explain what was happening. He believed that gravity causes an apple to fall, and then had the daring idea that gravity is a force that exists not only on Earth but throughout the whole Universe. Newton went on to prove this to be true in 1687, and scientists now use his ideas to predict the future of the Universe.

▼ The force of gravity acting on a rocket is related to its distance from the centre of the Earth. The pull of gravity falls very quickly as the rocket leaves Earth. At twice the distance from the Earth's centre, gravity is a quarter the strength it is on the Earth's surface.

at three times the distance, gravity is a ninth as strong as at the Earth's surface

at twice the distance from the Earth's centre, gravity is a quarter its strength on the Earth's surface

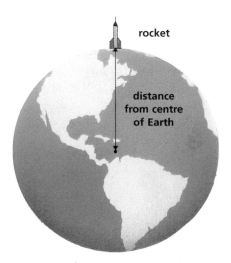

rocket

distance from centre of Earth

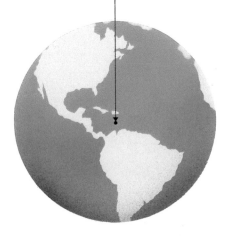

▶ If you drop one ball and throw another forward from the same height, both balls take exacly the same time to reach the ground. This is because both balls fall the same vertical distance.

▼ An astronaut floats in space high above the Earth. In space, an astronaut is weightless and is said to experience 'zero gravity'. However, gravity is not zero in space. It is still acting on the astronaut and causes him or her to move in an orbit around the Earth.

▼ Imagine standing on a tower high enough to be outside the Earth's atmosphere. If you threw a ball from the tower, gravity will pull it to Earth (a). But if you could throw the ball as fast as a rocket (b), the curve of its fall would match the curve of the Earth, and the ball would orbit the Earth.

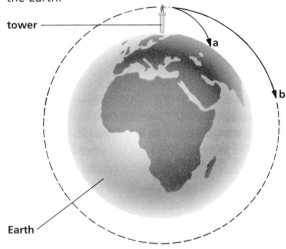

tower

Earth

Gaining and losing weight

Gravity gives everything its weight. The force of gravity between you and the Earth pulls you down, and your weight is the amount of force that you exert on the ground – or on a weighing machine.

However, if you were to fly to the Moon, you would weigh only a sixth of your Earth weight. This is because the Moon is much smaller than the Earth, and has only about a sixth of the Earth's gravity.

ROUND AND ROUND

Everything, everywhere, is moving. Out in space, satellites, moons, planets and stars are in non-stop motion. Inside the atoms that make up everything, tiny particles are moving non-stop, too. All these things move in the same way – in orbits.

An orbit is a circular or oval path around a centre of some kind. Man-made satellites and the Moon orbit around the Earth, while the Earth and other planets orbit the centre of the Solar System, the Sun. Stars, including the Sun, go round and round the centre of the group of stars which is called the Galaxy.

In every atom, one or more electrons go round the nucleus, a particle at the centre of the atom.

▶ Spacecraft meet in space high above the Earth as a new section called *Unity* (foreground) is added to the International Space Station (centre). The incoming spacecraft fires its rocket engines to go faster and so reach the same orbit as the station.

 key words

- orbit
- satellite

◀ Tie an object firmly to some string and whirl it around. You pull on the string to keep it in an orbit around your hand. Likewise, gravity between the Sun and Earth pulls on the Earth to keep it in orbit around the Sun.

A central pull

All orbiting things, from tiny electrons to huge stars, keep to their paths because a force comes from the centre and pulls them into an orbit. Out in space, this force is gravity. Inside atoms, this is electrical force.

Without these central forces, all the satellites, moons, planets and stars would leave their orbits and fly off into space. And all atoms would blow apart as electrons left their orbits.

Reaching orbit

Large rockets launch satellites and spacecraft into Earth's orbit. They must reach orbital velocity – a speed of 28,000 kilometres per hour – to stay in orbit, or they crash back to Earth. Once in orbit a satellite needs no power, because there is no air friction in space to slow it down.

At a speed of 40,000 kilometres per hour ('escape velocity') a spacecraft can escape from Earth's orbit altogether, and go into orbit around the Sun.

TELLING THE TIME

If you were born on 29 February, you are four years older on every birthday! You have only one birthday every four years. This is because of the way we measure time.

Units of time come from the Earth's movement. One day is the time it takes the Earth to make one turn on its axis. One year is the time it takes the Earth to travel once around the Sun. There are actually 365¼ days in one year. So every four years, we add an extra day (29 February) to make up the difference.

What's the time?

People divide the day into smaller units of time – hours, minutes and seconds. A day has 24 hours, an hour 60 minutes, and each minute 60 seconds. We use clocks and watches to keep track of hours, minutes and seconds.

Clocks and watches all work in the same basic way. A power source, usually a battery or spring, moves hands around a dial or lights up a display. A regulator controls the

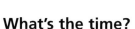

key words
- day
- time
- year

▲ Long ago, people used sundials to tell the time. The shadow of the pointer was like an hour hand. Sundials work because the shadow moves round the dial at the same rate as the Earth turns on its axis.

movement of the hands, or the change of numbers in the display, so that the clock or watch keeps good time. The regulator is a spring, pendulum or vibrating crystal that keeps a steady pace.

Scientists measure time very accurately using an atomic clock, which counts vibrations of atoms. It is so accurate that it would be only about one second out after working for a million years.

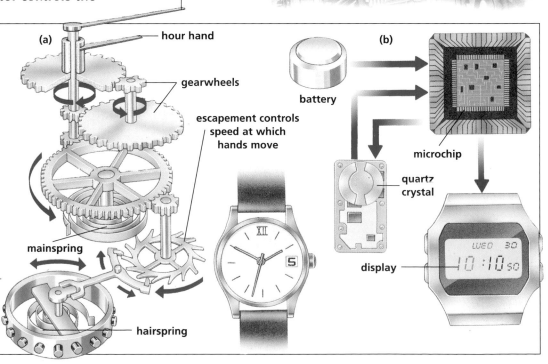

HOW CLOCKS AND WATCHES WORK

In a mechanical clock or watch, the power to move the hands comes from a coiled mainspring as it slowly unwinds. A small hairspring, which coils and uncoils at a regular rate, controls the speed at which the hands move, so that the clock or watch keeps good time.

In a digital clock or watch, a quartz crystal, powered by a battery, vibrates at thousands of times a second. This accurately controls the change of numbers in the display so that the watch shows the right time.

(a)

minute hand

hour hand

gearwheels

escapement controls speed at which hands move

mainspring

hairspring

(b)

battery

microchip

quartz crystal

display

SLOW TIME

If you could travel in a super-fast spacecraft at 99 per cent of the speed of light to the star Sirius and back, 17½ years would pass on Earth before you returned. But time would slow down on the journey. On your return, you would be only 2½ years older!

The theory of relativity says that, to an outside observer, time is seen to slow down for moving things. They have to move very fast – near to the speed of light (300,000 kilometres a second) – for time to slow very much. No spacecraft can move this fast, but fast-moving particles show that relativity really is true.

The ultimate speed limit

Time is not the only quantity to change for fast-moving things. To an outside observer the mass of an object increases as it moves faster, and its length decreases.

The theory of relativity says that the mass of an object would become infinitely great if it moved at the speed of light. Infinite mass is impossible. Therefore, nothing can move at or faster than the speed of light.

Creating energy

Relativity also explains that mass changes into energy. This means that a material can be destroyed and turn into energy, such as heat and light. It explains how the Sun

key words

- mass
- relativity
- speed of light
- time

▼ Einstein worked out his theory of relativity after it had been found that the speed of light is always the same, no matter how fast the person measuring it is moving. If the train driver and the person on the ground both measured the speed of the light coming from the signal, they would get the same result, even though the train is rushing towards the light.

shines. It produces immense heat because gas at its centre is changing into huge amounts of energy.

Nuclear reactors in nuclear power stations work in this way too. They convert a small amount of nuclear fuel into a huge amount of heat energy. The heat is then used to generate electricity.

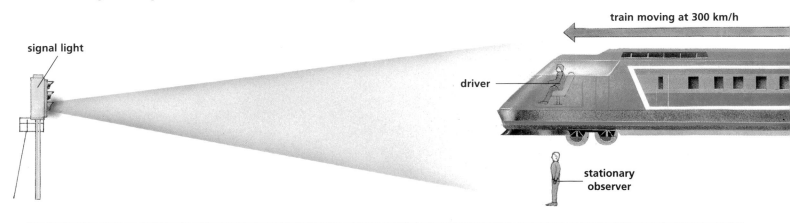

signal light

train moving at 300 km/h

driver

stationary observer

HOT AND COLD

If you hold the wooden handle of a spade, and then touch the metal, the metal feels colder than the wood, even though the two materials are really the same temperature. This is because of the way heat flows.

Your fingertips are warmer than the metal. Heat flows easily into the metal from them, because metal is a good conductor. As they lose heat, your fingertips get cooler and they feel cold. Heat does not flow easily into wood, which is a poor conductor. That's why your fingertips stay warm when they touch it.

HOW HEAT FLOWS

In a kitchen, heat usually comes from burning gas or electricity. The heat has to flow into food to cook it. Heat flows in three ways – conduction, convection and radiation.

Heat from a gas flame or electric hotplate enters the base of the saucepan. It flows through the metal, and into the water in the pan, by conduction.

Heat flows through the water by convection. Currents of hot water rise from the base of the pan and carry heat to all the water.

Red-hot wires heated by electricity toast bread in a toaster. The hot wire gives out heat rays that heat everything they meet. This kind of heat flow is called radiation.

Gain and loss

Heat is a form of energy, and everything has a certain amount of heat. An object gets hotter if heat flows into it and it gains more heat. If heat flows away, an object gets colder.

Everything is made of atoms and molecules that are moving. When heat flows into something, it makes these particles move faster. When heat is lost, they slow down.

▲ Most materials contract when they get colder, but water expands as it freezes to ice. This makes ice less dense than water, which causes ice to float in water, like this iceberg.

Heating up

Rub your hands together quickly: they soon feel warm. The friction makes the particles in your skin speed up, and it gets hotter. Striking a match produces enough heat in this way to cause the head of the match to burst into flame.

The Sun is our main source of heat. Heat rays radiate out from the Sun. Solar heating systems store the Sun's heat and use it to warm buildings and heat water.

key words
- contraction
- expansion
- heat

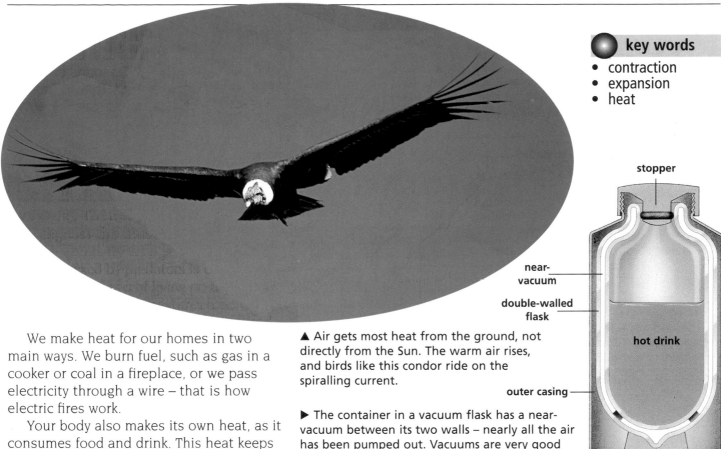

stopper

near-vacuum

double-walled flask

hot drink

outer casing

We make heat for our homes in two main ways. We burn fuel, such as gas in a cooker or coal in a fireplace, or we pass electricity through a wire – that is how electric fires work.

Your body also makes its own heat, as it consumes food and drink. This heat keeps you warm and keeps your body working.

Bigger and smaller

Heat not only makes particles move faster. It also makes them move apart, which is why a heated object expands. When Concorde is flying, its hull gets very hot and expands by about 25 centimetres!

In the same way, when something gets colder, the particles slow down and move together, so the object contracts and gets smaller.

Heating a container of gas raises its pressure as the gas particles move faster and strike the container walls with greater force. A car engine burns fuel to make hot gases, and the hot, high-pressure gases drive the engine's moving parts. A jet plane's engine works in the same way. Both of these types of engine are known as heat engines.

▲ Air gets most heat from the ground, not directly from the Sun. The warm air rises, and birds like this condor ride on the spiralling current.

▶ The container in a vacuum flask has a near-vacuum between its two walls – nearly all the air has been pumped out. Vacuums are very good insulators, so little heat can get in or out.

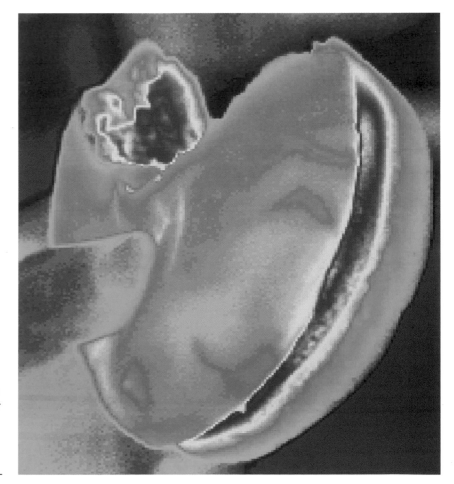

▶ In this thermograph (heat picture) of a person holding a burger, hotter and colder parts appear in different colours. The hottest parts, such as the burger itself, show up red. Parts coloured blue or purple, such as the bun, are the coldest.

HOW HOT?

Why do you shiver when it's cold, and sweat when it's hot? It is your body's way of keeping itself at the same steady temperature. If your temperature changes too much, you feel ill.

When you measure temperature, the number of degrees tells you how hot or how cold something is. If you are well, your body temperature is about 37°C (degrees Celsius or Centigrade). Shivering makes you warmer, and helps to stop your temperature falling lower in cold weather. Sweating cools you down, and stops your body from overheating.

By degrees

A temperature of 37°C is warm. Ice is cold and has a temperature of 0°C, while boiling water has a temperature of 100°C.

Temperatures in degrees Celsius or Centigrade are on the Celsius scale. There is another scale called the Fahrenheit scale. Ice has a temperature of 32°F (degrees Fahrenheit), your body 98°F, and boiling water 212°F.

Thermometers measure temperature. A glass thermometer contains a thin tube in which a liquid moves up and down a scale of degrees to show the temperature. This liquid is usually mercury or coloured alcohol. The liquid rises when it is warmed and drops when cooled. A digital thermometer has a screen that displays the number of degrees.

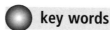

key words

- Celsius
- centigrade
- Fahrenheit
- temperature
- thermometer
- thermostat

▶ Temperatures range from absolute zero, the lowest possible temperature, up to temperatures of millions of degrees inside the Sun and other stars. Substances freeze, melt or boil at set temperatures.

◀ A clinical thermometer is a special glass thermometer used to measure body temperature. It has a small range of temperature a few degrees above and below normal, which is about 37°C or 98°F.

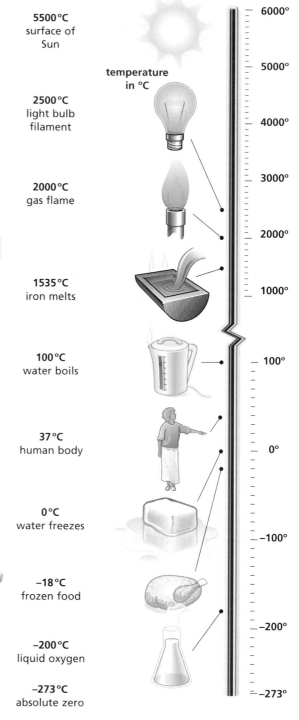

temperature in °C

| 5500°C surface of Sun |
| 2500°C light bulb filament |
| 2000°C gas flame |
| 1535°C iron melts |
| 100°C water boils |
| 37°C human body |
| 0°C water freezes |
| −18°C frozen food |
| −200°C liquid oxygen |
| −273°C absolute zero |

6000°
5000°
4000°
3000°
2000°
1000°
100°
0°
−100°
−200°
−273°

Keeping warm

A heating system keeps the rooms of a house at a comfortable temperature. It contains devices called thermostats that detect and control the room temperature. The thermostat switches the heating on if the room is too cool, and off when it gets too hot.

Electric kettles also have thermostats. They switch the kettle off when the water gets to the temperature at which it boils.

KEEPING COOL

Wet your finger and blow on it. Your finger gets cold before it dries. Refrigerators work in a similar way to keep food and drinks cool.

Blowing air over a wet finger makes the water quickly evaporate or dry up. Water loses heat as it evaporates. It takes this heat from your finger, which gets colder.

Refrigerators and freezers use evaporation to remove heat from food and drinks. A refrigerator cools food and drinks to a temperature just above freezing. This keeps them fresh for a few days, because bacteria do not multiply so fast at low temperatures, so the food does not decay. In a freezer, food is frozen to a temperature of about −18°C, and this preserves it for a long time, because bacteria cannot multiply at all below freezing.

How a refrigerator works

Inside a refrigerator is a tube containing a liquid called a refrigerant. The liquid

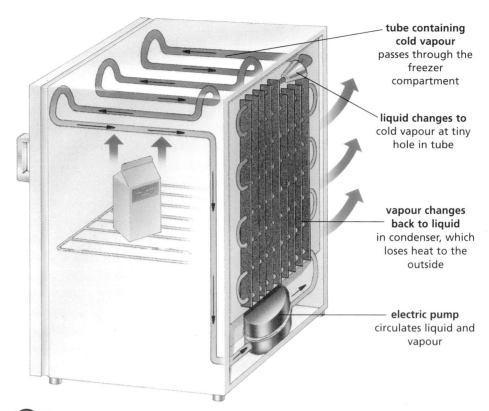

tube containing cold vapour passes through the freezer compartment

liquid changes to cold vapour at tiny hole in tube

vapour changes back to liquid in condenser, which loses heat to the outside

electric pump circulates liquid and vapour

key words
- evaporation
- liquid
- refrigerant
- vapour

▼ The cold tubes of a refrigeration system pass through the base of an ice rink to keep the ice frozen.

▲ A refrigerator takes heat from inside the freezer compartment, and transfers it to the warm condenser outside. Cold air descends from the freezer compartment to cool the whole interior.

passes through a tiny hole inside the tube, which makes it evaporate and become a vapour. It gets very cold, and takes heat from inside the refrigerator so that the contents are cooled.

The tube, now containing cold vapour, goes to the rear of the refrigerator. The refrigerant changes back into a liquid, which makes it gain heat. The heat taken from the food warms the tube, which is why the back of the refrigerator is warm. Then the liquid refrigerant returns to the inside to evaporate and cool again.

Freezers and air conditioning units work in the same way as refrigerators.

Cryogenics is the study of very low temperatures. Some materials become superconductors when extremely cold. They lose all electrical resistance and can conduct very strong electrical currents.

BURNING BRIGHT

If you could take the energy from just one litre of petrol and use it to power yourself, then you would be able to cycle over 500 kilometres! Petrol is just one of several energy-rich fuels that we use to produce power.

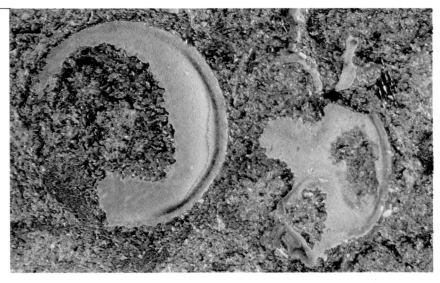

▲ In this slice of coal, the yellow areas are the leaves of some of the plants that formed the coal.

Just about every time you switch on a light, use a heater, cooker or a powered machine, or take a ride in a car, bus, train or plane, you are causing fuel to burn.

We depend on machines like these, so we need an abundant source of energy to power them. Fuels are the most useful energy source we have. They contain a lot of energy that we can release as heat energy simply by burning them. Fuels provide much more energy than other energy sources such as solar power and wind power.

1 Oil and gas formed from tiny sea creatures that died millions of years ago. and sank to the seabed.

2 Layers of rock gradually built up over the sea creatures. Heat and pressure under the earth changed their remains into liquid oil and gas.

1 The forests that formed coal grew in the Carboniferous Period, about 300 million years ago. In swampy areas, the trees and plants decayed very slowly.

2 The rotting plants formed a layer of spongy material called peat.

3 The peat was slowly buried under layers of mud and sand. It formed a soft coal called lignite.

▶ Coal, oil and gas are known as fossil fuels because they are the remains of things that lived millions of years ago. Coal is the remains of ancient forests that grew millions of years ago. Oil and gas are found where there were seas long ago.

4 After millions of years underground, the lignite was squashed into layers of hard coal.

Heat is power

Some heaters and cookers burn fuel like gas to make and use heat directly. Cars and most other kinds of transport have engines that burn petrol or other fuel. Even electric trains, lights and other electrical machines use fuel – the electricity that powers them comes mostly from power stations that burn fuel such as coal.

The main fuels are coal, crude oil or petroleum, and natural gas. These are known as fossil fuels. Petrol and diesel for engines come from crude oil.

Another important fuel is nuclear fuel. It produces huge amounts of heat energy, and is used in nuclear power stations to generate electricity.

An energy-hungry world

We burn fuels in huge quantities, but this produces smoke, fumes and waste gases that pollute the air, causing illness and damaging buildings. One product of burning fuels is carbon dioxide, an invisible gas that enters the atmosphere. Rising levels of carbon dioxide are causing global warming, a gradual rise in temperature at the Earth's surface that could bring about serious damage in the future.

The waste from nuclear fuel is very dangerous to health, and storing this waste is also a cause for concern.

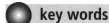

THE FUTURE OF FUEL

Fuels come from deposits underground, which will eventually run out. Although new deposits may be found in the future, it makes sense to try to use up less fuel so that the deposits will last longer.

Using cars with smaller engines, and insulating houses to reduce heat losses, are two good ways of cutting back on fuels. Using less fuel also helps to reduce pollution and global warming.

We can also tackle the problem by finding alternative sources of fuel. Renewable resources include energy from the Sun, which will not run out for another 4500 million years.

▼ In hot countries, people may collect cow dung and then dry it in the Sun to produce a fuel.

3 The liquid oil and gas slowly moved upwards through tiny holes in the rocks above them.

4 Eventually the oil and gas reached a rock layer that they could not pass through, and deposits collected.

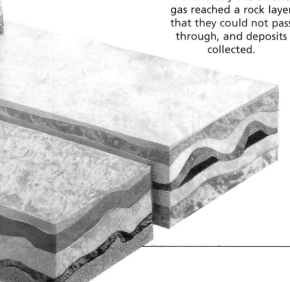

SOLID FUEL

A century ago, many cities were full of grimy, dark, black buildings. They were coated with soot – black powder from the smoke from coal fires. Nowadays, cities are much cleaner as smoke no longer fills the air. But coal remains an important fuel.

Coal is a hard, black substance made of carbon. It catches fire and burns fiercely when strongly heated. It is found in deposits underground and at the surface of the ground. Coal formed over millions of years from the remains of trees and plants.

Peat is coal at an early stage of its formation. It is brown and softer than coal, and is found at the surface, not deep underground.

Mining coal

If the deposits of coal are at or near the surface of the ground, the coal is dug out in

key words
- bitumen
- coke
- opencast
- steam engine

▲ This massive excavator cuts coal from a huge opencast mine.

vast pits called opencast mines. Huge excavating machines strip off any soil covering the coal, and dig out the coal beneath.

Coal often lies in seams or layers deep underground. At underground mines, shafts go down to the seams. Miners take lifts down to the seams, and then dig tunnels through the seams as they remove the coal. They use cutting machines to dig out the coal. Conveyor belts take the coal back to the shafts, where lifts raise it to the surface buildings.

Industrial power

Coal brought the people of the 17th and early 18th centuries comfort at home, the means to travel widely, and lots of useful goods and products. It powered steam locomotives on railways, and ocean-going passenger ships. Factories burned coal to power steam engines and to produce heat for manufacturing products. People used coal and peat to heat their homes, burning them in open fires that could also heat running water for warm baths.

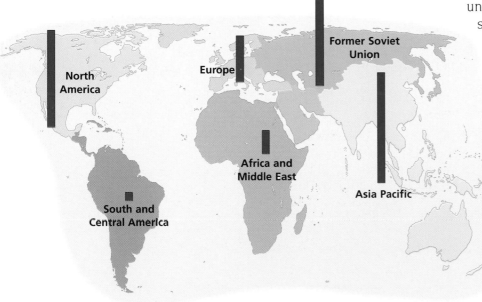

North America

Europe

Former Soviet Union

Africa and Middle East

Asia Pacific

South and Central America

▲ This map shows the world's known reserves of coal. Europe (including the former Soviet Union) has about a third of the world's coal, while North America and Asia each have about a quarter. These reserves should last for several hundred years.

Key to map
■ coal reserves

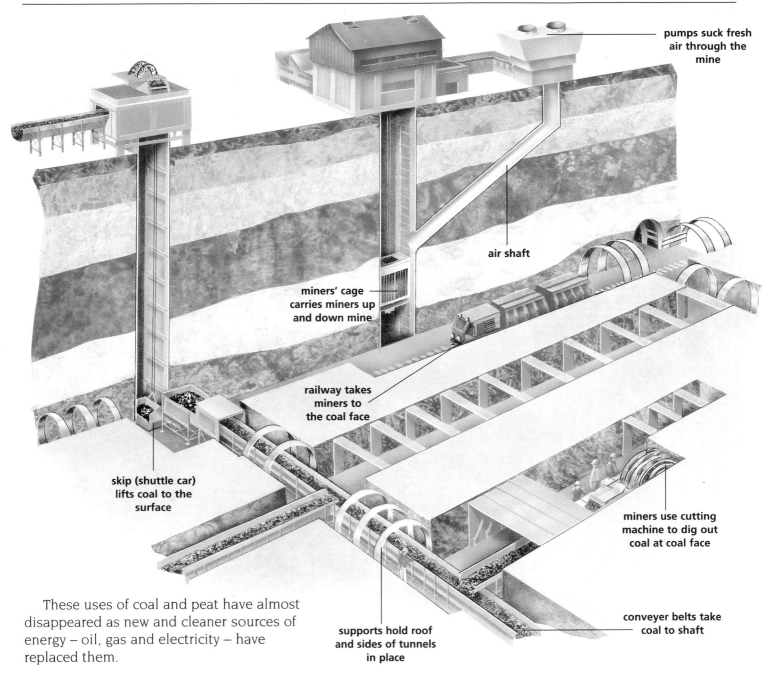

pumps suck fresh air through the mine

air shaft

miners' cage carries miners up and down mine

railway takes miners to the coal face

skip (shuttle car) lifts coal to the surface

miners use cutting machine to dig out coal at coal face

conveyer belts take coal to shaft

supports hold roof and sides of tunnels in place

These uses of coal and peat have almost disappeared as new and cleaner sources of energy – oil, gas and electricity – have replaced them.

Useful products

Peat is now used mainly for growing garden plants, but coal is still an important source of power. Many power stations burn coal to raise steam to drive electricity generators. Factories making products such as cement burn coal to provide the heat for the manufacturing process.

Coal also provides useful products for industry. Heating coal without air produces coke, which is used to make steel. Bitumen for surfacing roads comes from coal, and coal also contains chemicals used to make dyes, drugs and plastics.

▲ An underground coal mine is a maze of tunnels. Some lead from the main shaft to the seams or layers of coal. Other tunnels are formed as the miners cut away the coal deposits. The tunnels may be many kilometres long: in coastal areas, they may extend out under the seabed.

Did you know that you can use coal products to wash yourself? Coal is not only used as a fuel. Coal is also a source of chemicals that can be processed to make soap and dyes, as well as medicines, pesticides and other products.

BLACK GOLD

If you could dig deep, far below the ground you might find a liquid, so dark and so precious that it is sometimes called 'black gold'. It is crude oil. It is a valuable fuel that powers transport and machines, and it also contains a whole range of useful chemicals.

Crude oil, often called petroleum or simply oil, lies sealed in cavities in rock deep under the land and under the seabed. In these deposits, there may also be large quantities of natural gas, mainly methane.

Oil and gas deposits formed over millions of years from the buried remains of animals and plants that lived in ancient seas.

key words

- gas
- oil
- refinery
- rig
- terminal

Drilling for oil

Experts search for deposits of oil and gas by studying the layers of rock deep beneath the land and seabed. They locate cavities where deposits are likely to lie. But the only way to be sure is to drill for oil or gas.

On land, a drilling rig is set up. This lowers a sharp drill into the ground. In soft ground, the drill can dig down 60 metres every hour.

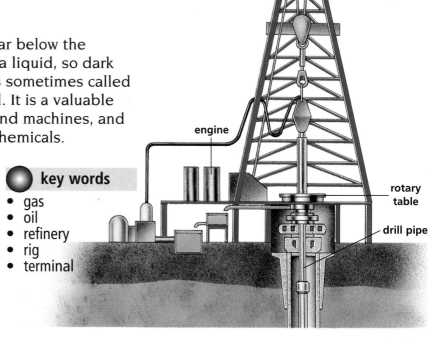

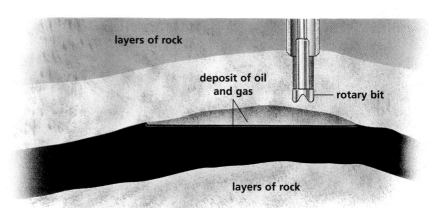

▲ An oil rig drills a deep shaft into the ground to find a deposit of oil or gas. The deposit may be hundreds of metres down.

At sea, a drilling rig is built on tall legs that go down to the seabed. If the water is too deep, the rig floats at the surface. The rig sends a drill down through the water to the seabed, and drills down into it.

◄ Saudi Arabia and other countries of the Middle East have almost half the world's known reserves of oil. The United States has about 20 per cent and Europe, including Russia, about 15 per cent. These reserves are expected to last for about 50 more years.

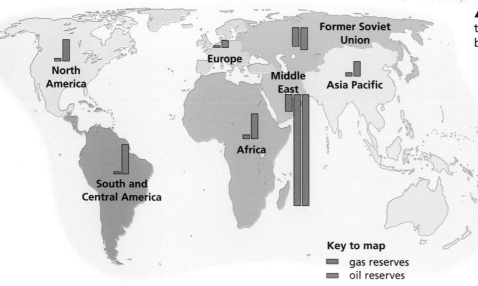

Key to map
- gas reserves
- oil reserves

Striking oil

If the drill meets a deposit, the oil or gas flows back up the shaft or is pumped up. The shaft becomes an oil well or gas well.

On land, the oil rig is taken down and the top of the well is fitted with pipes to take the oil or gas away. At sea, the rig is removed and a production platform towed out to the drilling site. This may be a huge tower that stands on the seabed and supports a platform above the water. Or the production platform may float. Pipes go down from the platform to the oil well on the seabed.

▼ At an oil refinery the crude oil is separated into many different products. The main ones are fuels (such as liquid petroleum gas (LPG), petrol, paraffin and diesel), lubricating oils, and bitumen for surfacing roads.

▲ Oil deep below the seabed flows up shafts to a production platform. There the oil is treated to remove water and also waste gas, which may burn off in a flare. The oil is piped or sent by tanker to a refinery, which may also receive oil pumped up from oil wells on land.

Using oil and gas

Tankers and pipelines carry the oil to oil refineries. The crude oil contains lots of useful substances, including diesel, petrol and kerosene. At the refinery, these different substances are separated out.

Tankers and pipes take gas to gas terminals, too. There the gas is purified and then piped direct to homes and factories, or bottled for use in places with no direct gas supply. In homes, gas is used for cooking and heating. It is also used as a source of heat for industry, and some power stations burn gas to produce electricity.

▶ After refining, products such as liquid petroleum gas (LPG) and petrol are stored in huge tanks before being pumped into road tankers, oil drums or canisters for delivery.

The world's production of oil is about 27,000 million barrels per year (one barrel is 159 litres of oil). This is enough oil to fill approximately 10 million public swimming pools.

TAMING WATERFALLS

The sight of a mighty waterfall like Niagara Falls is awesome. The water roars as it strikes the river or rocks far below. Can such enormous power be harnessed? In fact, a fifth of the world's electricity comes from water power.

Not all power stations burn fuel. The most powerful ones are hydroelectric, which means they generate electricity from water. The power station at the Itaipu Dam on the River Paraná, Paraguay, for example, generates over 12,500 megawatts of electricity – twice as much as the biggest coal-powered plants.

Hydroelectric power stations do not use up the water or turn it into something else. Flowing or falling water has energy, and a hydroelectric station changes some of the energy into electricity. When the water comes out of the power station, it moves less fast, because it has given up some of its energy.

key words
- hydroelectric
- pumped storage
- tidal power

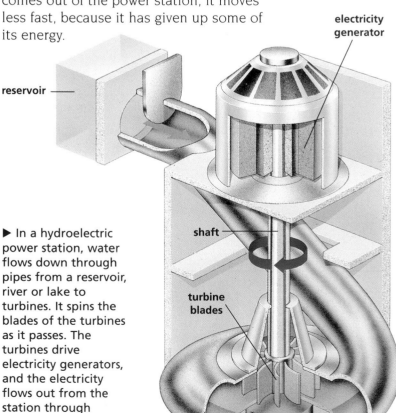

▶ In a hydroelectric power station, water flows down through pipes from a reservoir, river or lake to turbines. It spins the blades of the turbines as it passes. The turbines drive electricity generators, and the electricity flows out from the station through power lines.

reservoir
electricity generator
shaft
turbine blades
water

▲ A waterwheel turns as water flows from a channel over the blades mounted on the wheel. The turbines in hydroelectric power stations work in the same basic way, but produce more power.

Electricity from water

High dams are built across river valleys to create large reservoirs or artificial lakes that can supply people with water. A dam may contain a hydroelectric power station. Water from the reservoir flows down through the dam to drive the station's turbines, which in turn drive generators that produce electricity.

Hydroelectric stations are also built without high dams. They take water from fast-flowing rivers or are fed with water piped down from high lakes.

Many rivers flow too slowly to be used for generating electricity, or their valleys are not deep enough to be dammed. Hydroelectric stations are built mainly in mountainous regions with heavy rainfall, such as Switzerland, Norway, Sweden and

THE THREE GORGES DAM
The world's largest hydroelectric project is under construction in the region of the Three Gorges on the Yangtze River, China. Plans call for a dam 185 metres high and 2 kilometres long to create a reservoir extending 600 kilometres along the valley. When completed in 2009, the dam will generate about 18,000 megawatts of electricity – about 10 per cent of China's total electricity needs. But the project will drown 19 cities and displace almost 2 million people.

► At the mouth of the River Rance in northern France is a tidal power station. As the tide rises and falls, water flows rapidly into and out of the river. The water passes through turbines in a barrier across the river, and the turbines drive electricity generators. The power station generates 240 megawatts of electricity.

In 1968, the building of the Aswan High Dam in Egypt began to create a large lake that would drown the ancient temple at Abu Simbel. So, before the lake rose, the whole temple and its magnificent statues were cut out of the rock and rebuilt above the final water line.

Canada. Some large rivers have been dammed to provide power and also to prevent the rivers from flooding. These great dams include the Aswan High Dam across the River Nile in Egypt, and the Three Gorges Dam across the River Yangtze in China.

Clean and everlasting

Water power is a clean source of power. Unlike the burning of fuels, tapping the energy in flowing water does not pollute the air and cause global warming.

Furthermore, hydroelectric power stations are not using up a valuable source of energy. The water in rivers and lakes is constantly replaced by fresh rain.

Hydroelectric power stations produce about 20 per cent of the world's electricity. Building more hydroelectric stations would save fuel and reduce pollution and global warming. However, building in mountainous regions is difficult and costly.

Much of electricity generated there would be lost as it would have to travel a long way to cities. Most large rivers are not suitable for damming, and the creation of large reservoirs can cause hardship to the people who have to move away from the land that is to be drowned.

◄ The generator hall of the hydroelectric power station at Hoover Dam, USA. The huge electricity generators are driven by water turbines below the floor of the hall.

FUTURE POWER

In a tiny desert village in Rajasthan, India, an ordinary-looking lamp post shows how energy use is changing. This village has no electricity supply, but the lamp stores the Sun's energy by day to light the village at night. In the future, all people will need everlasting sources of energy like this.

We need energy sources to power all our machines and for cooking and heating in our homes. The Sun's energy, or solar energy, is one of several renewable energy sources that produce energy all the time.

At present we mainly use fuels to produce energy. Once burned, fuels are finished – they are not renewable. Our sources of fuel will run out in the future, and people will then depend on renewable energy.

Energy crisis

The world's known reserves of oil and gas are likely to run out by 2050. Today's nuclear power stations may have closed by then. Few new nuclear power stations are

▼ This experimental car is powered by the Sun. It is covered with solar cells that use sunlight to generate electricity and power the car's electric motor. Solar cells are likely to become an important source of energy in the future.

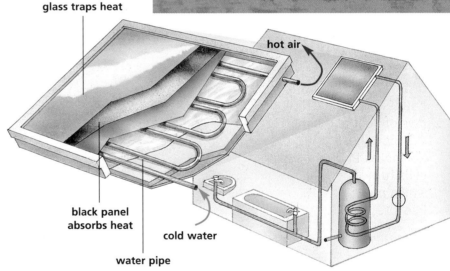

glass traps heat

hot air

black panel absorbs heat

cold water

water pipe

▲ Inside a solar heating panel is a layer of black material, which gets hot when the Sun shines on it. The material heats water flowing through a pipe in the panel. The hot water goes to heat the house or supply hot water to taps. Using solar heating cuts electricity or fuel costs.

being built, as many people consider them too dangerous, although scientists hope that power from nuclear fusion will soon be a reality. Coal will remain the only available fuel, and it could be used to make other fuels such as petrol. Known coal reserves will last for hundreds of years.

Using more renewable energy will cut back on fuel and make reserves last longer. Unlike fuels, renewable energy does not cause pollution and global warming, and it will reduce this damage too.

Everlasting energy

There are five main kinds of renewable resources. Hydroelectric power stations,

◄ This wind farm has rows of giant turbines. The wind spins the blades of each rotor, which drives an electricity generator at its hub. The photo has been 'cross-processed' to show the structure of the turbines more clearly.

key words

- geothermal power
- hydroelectric power
- solar power
- wave power
- wind power

More to come

Renewable resources do not produce much energy and are unlikely ever to meet all our energy needs. The International Energy Agency has forecast that by 2010, 3 per cent of all our energy will come from hydroelectric power and only 1 per cent from other renewable resources. Coal, oil and gas will provide 90 per cent of our energy.

One reason for this is that generating electricity by solar power is costly. But as the fuels needed to produce electricity become rarer, they will also be more expensive. Then the use of solar power should increase.

which generate electricity from flowing water, produce the most energy.

Solar power taps the Sun's energy in two ways. Solar panels, often on roofs of houses, face the Sun and absorb solar rays of heat and light. Some panels tap the Sun's heat to warm a house or provide hot water. Photovoltaic panels or solar cells turn the Sun's rays into electricity, which may be stored in a battery for use later.

Geothermal power taps the energy inside the Earth. In some places, underground rocks are very hot. Water is heated by piping it through the hot rocks. In Iceland, most homes are heated in this way.

Wind turbines tap the energy of moving air. The wind turns the blades of the turbine, which drive an electricity generator. Wind turbines line high ridges or coasts in windy regions. Wind power is being used in many countries, particularly Germany, India, Denmark and Spain.

Wave machines of various kinds tap the energy of water as it rises and falls in waves and convert the energy into electricity. This renewable resource is still undergoing development.

▼ Geothermal power stations may be built where hot rocks lie close to the surface, for example in volcanic regions. Hot water in the rocks is brought to the surface through a bore hole. There the hot steam drives steam turbines that power electricity generators.

electricity generator

steam turbine

steam separator

steam cools to water

hot water rises through bore hole

cold water returned to ground

cooling tower

POWER PRODUCTION

Have you ever had a machine in your mouth? You probably have – when you were at the dentist's. Inside a dentist's drill is a tiny turbine whizzing round thousands of times a second. It is powered by a stream of air.

Engines, turbines and motors drive most machines and make parts move. Engines burn fuel, while turbines require moving air, steam or water.

Heat engines

Most engines use heat. They burn fuel, such as petrol, in air they suck in. The hot gases produced expand rapidly, and make the parts of the engine move. Petrol and diesel engines in road vehicles and trains, and jet engines in aircraft, work in this way. All these engines are called internal-combustion engines as they burn fuel inside the engine.

In steam engines, hot steam drives the moving parts. Fuel is burned in boilers outside the engine to produce the steam, so these engines are called external-combustion engines.

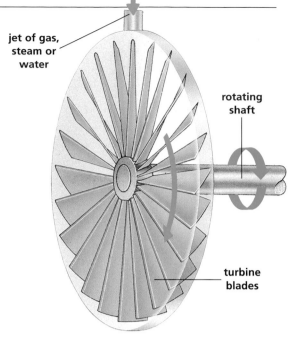

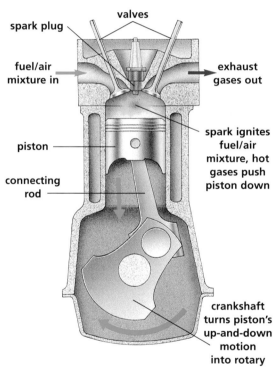

> ● **key words**
> • external-combustion engine
> • internal combustion engine
> • piston engine
> • turbine

▶ A turbine (top) produces circular or rotary motion directly. A piston engine (bottom) produces up-and-down motion, which is changed into rotary motion by the crankshaft.

Turbines

A turbine works rather like an old windmill or waterwheel. It has blades that spin round when driven by a moving gas or liquid. Wind turbines use moving air, and water turbines in hydroelectric power stations are driven by moving water. Steam turbines in other power stations are driven by heated steam.

◀ The jet engine of an aircraft is a gas turbine. The blades of the turbine can be seen in the centre of the picture.

ON THE BOIL

You boil a kettle of water to make a cup of tea or coffee – power stations boil water on a far greater scale. This generates the supply of electricity that comes to your home and makes your kettle work.

When water boils, it produces a large amount of hot steam. This steam has a lot of energy. Most power stations burn fuel to boil water, and the hot steam goes to huge steam turbines that drive the generators.

 key words
- piston engine
- steam locomotive
- steam turbine

STEAM POWER

The steam engine was developed into a powerful, efficient engine by the British engineer James Watt (1736–1819) in 1769. He improved a slow and inefficient engine invented in 1712 by Thomas Newcomen. Units of power are called watts in honour of his achievement.

Steam turbines

Inside the turbine are sets of blades fixed to a central shaft. The steam drives the blades around, turning the shaft with great power. The turbine shaft drives an electric generator, and the electricity flows through power lines to homes.

Some large ships are powered by steam turbines, which drive the ship's propellers.

Steam trains

The steam engines in old locomotives were piston engines. A coal-fired boiler in the locomotive raised steam, which went to cylinders by the wheels. Inside each cylinder, the steam pushed a piston backwards and forwards and the piston drove a connecting rod and crankshaft that turned the wheels.

Steam piston engines once powered factories and ships, too.

◀ The fastest steam locomotive was *Mallard*, which reached a record speed of 203 kilometres per hour in 1938. It is now in the National Rail Museum in York, England.

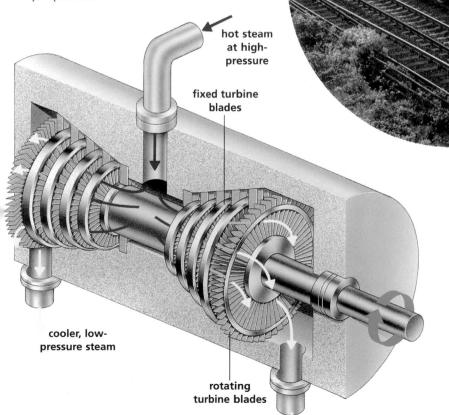

hot steam at high-pressure

fixed turbine blades

cooler, low-pressure steam

rotating turbine blades

A steam turbine can produce a huge amount of power. A large steam turbine generates as much power as all the engines in about 20,000 family cars.

◀ The steam turbine in a power station has several sets of blades all fixed to a central shaft. The steam enters the first set at high pressure and, having turned the blades, leaves at lower pressure. The next sets of blades work at lower pressure. In this way, the turbine uses up nearly all of the energy in the hot steam.

PACKING A PUNCH

Foresters need chainsaws that are powerful enough to cut down big trees, but also light and portable. Only one kind of engine is suitable for the saw – a petrol engine. It carries its own fuel supply and is light yet powerful.

Petrol and diesel engines power all sorts of vehicles, from cars and motorcycles to diesel trains, boats and small aircraft. Being light and portable, petrol engines are also used to drive machines such as lawnmowers and chainsaws.

Inside a petrol engine

A petrol engine contains one or more cylinders in which a piston moves up and down. It produces power by burning petrol in the cylinders. The intense heat causes air in the cylinders to expand violently, driving down the pistons. The pistons turn a crankshaft, which drives the wheels, propeller or other mechanism.

The petrol engine in a car is a four-stroke engine. The piston repeats a cycle of four movements in which it goes up and

▲ A chainsaw has a rotating chain lined with sharp teeth that cuts into the wood. It is driven by a small but powerful petrol engine, and can cut through a thick trunk or branch quickly and easily.

down twice. Motorcycles and other light machines often have simpler, two-stroke engines. The piston repeats a cycle in which it goes up and down once.

Diesel engines

A diesel engine works in the same way as a petrol engine, except that it needs no spark plug to ignite the fuel. The air is strongly compressed, which causes it to heat up. Fuel is then added, and it immediately ignites in the hot air.

key words

- catalytic converter
- diesel engine
- four-stroke
- petrol engine
- two-stroke

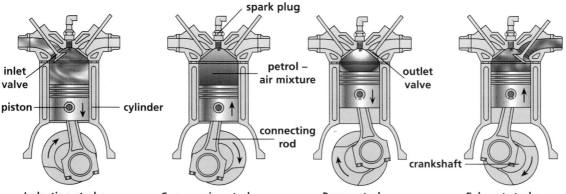

Induction stroke.
On the first stroke, the piston goes down and sucks air into the cylinder through the inlet valve.

Compression stroke.
On the second stroke, the fuel injector squirts petrol into the cylinder as the piston rises and compresses the petrol – air mixture.

Power stroke.
The spark plug ignites the compressed mixture. The hot gases produced expand and force down the piston on its third, power stroke.

Exhaust stroke.
On the fourth stroke, the piston rises and pushes the waste gases out of the cylinder through the outlet valve.

◄ A four-stroke petrol engine repeats a cycle of four strokes, or movements, in which the piston goes up and down the cylinder twice. Car engines usually have four cylinders, each on a different stroke at any time.

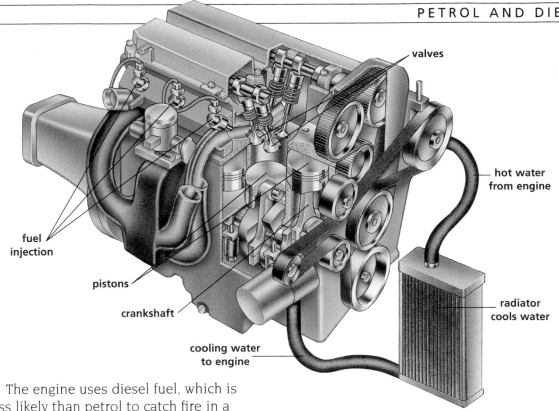

valves

fuel
injection

pistons

crankshaft

cooling water
to engine

hot water
from engine

radiator
cools water

The German engineer Rudolf Diesel developed the diesel engine. He patented his invention in 1892.

◄ A diesel engine has no spark plugs. Instead, the injected fuel is compressed until it is hot enough to ignite by itself.

The engine uses diesel fuel, which is less likely than petrol to catch fire in a crash. Diesel engines are simpler in construction, more robust and more fuel-efficient. Unfortunately, they cause more pollution than petrol engines.

Outside the engine

Around a petrol or diesel engine are several systems that make the engine work.

The injection system controls the supply of fuel to the cylinders, squirting in more when the vehicle needs to go faster. In petrol engines, the ignition system makes the fuel ignite at the right moment to give the most power.

The exhaust system leads waste gases away from the cylinders into the atmosphere. The fuel ignites with a bang, and the exhaust system has a silencer that reduces this noise. The waste gases are polluting, and the catalytic converter in the exhaust system makes most of the polluting gases harmless. It does not remove carbon dioxide, though, which causes global warming.

▼ In Thailand, many boats have a petrol or diesel engine and propeller mounted at the end of a long steering handle. This makes it easy to turn the boat quickly. However, the boats are very noisy.

POWER IN THE AIR

▼ B-58 bomber. Flames roar from the engine of this jet fighter. They come from the afterburner, which burns more fuel in the exhaust to increase power when needed.

Only two centuries ago, it could have taken you a whole day to travel to the nearest city – the fastest stagecoach could not top 300 kilometres in a day. Nowadays, an airliner covers this distance in 20 minutes! Every large city in the world is no more than a day's journey away.

Most airliners cruise at speeds of up to about 1000 kilometres per hour. Supersonic aircraft can travel up to three times as fast. The jet engine makes economical high-speed travel possible. It produces great power without being very heavy.

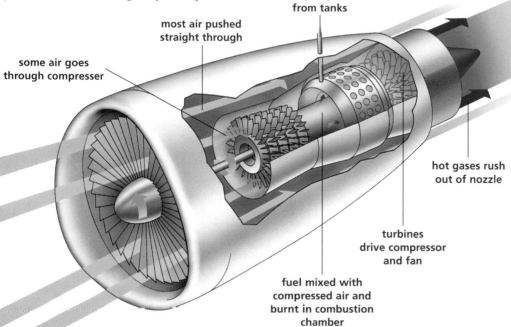

fuel pumped in from tanks

most air pushed straight through

some air goes through compresser

hot gases rush out of nozzle

turbines drive compressor and fan

fuel mixed with compressed air and burnt in combustion chamber

◄ Inside a turbofan jet engine. A huge fan sucks in air. Turbofan engines are much more efficient than turbojets. Some of the air is compressed, then heated in the combustion chamber to increase the pressure even more. This jet of hot air then shoots out of the back of the engine, turning a turbine to power the compresser and the fan as it goes. The rest of the air drawn in by the fan goes around the chamber and out of the back adding an extra 'push' of cooler air.

How a jet engine works

There are three main types of jet engines – turbojets, turbofans and turboprops. A turbojet engine is the basic model. It sucks in air at the front, burns fuel to heat the air, and expels the hot gases from the rear of the engine. The gases leave the engine in a powerful jet, thrusting the engine – and the aircraft– forwards with a strong force.

These days, most airliners use turbofan engines, in which a large outer shell surrounds the jet engine. A turbofan engine produces more power because more air flows through it. The shell surrounding the engine also makes it less noisy. Turboprop engines are often used in helicopters. The turbine drives a shaft connected to the rotors.

key words
- compressor
- turbine
- turbofan

THE WAY TO SPACE

The most exciting part of a firework display comes as rockets zoom up into the night sky and burst high above in cascades of colour. All spacecraft get to space and travel there in the same way. Only a rocket engine can carry them up and out into space.

The rocket engines of a spacecraft, such as the space shuttle, work in the same way as a firework rocket. They both burn fuel called a propellant very quickly to produce huge amounts of hot gases. As these gases rush out from the exhaust of the engine or tail of the rocket, they exert a powerful force on the engine or rocket and drive it forwards or upwards.

Beyond the air

Most kinds of transport have engines that burn fuels, such as

▶ The *Ariane* rocket is a huge rocket that launches a payload such as a satellite into space. It has three sections called stages that fire in turn. When its fuel is used up, each stage falls away and the next stage takes over. Only the payload and third stage reach space. Using stages saves fuel.

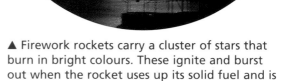

▲ Firework rockets carry a cluster of stars that burn in bright colours. These ignite and burst out when the rocket uses up its solid fuel and is high in the air.

petrol, diesel fuel or paraffin. Fuels need a gas called oxygen to catch fire and burn. This oxygen comes from the air.

Rockets are different. They carry their own oxygen, and so can work beyond the atmosphere where there is no air.

Rocket fuels

Firework rockets and many space rockets that launch spacecraft use fuel made of powder. In this solid fuel is a substance containing oxygen, which enables the fuel to burn. A solid-fuel rocket engine continues to burn until the fuel is used up.

In all spacecraft and many rocket launchers, two liquids are pumped to the engine, where they catch fire and burn. In most liquid-fuel engines, one liquid is liquid oxygen and the other is a liquid fuel such as liquid hydrogen.

Liquid-fuel rocket engines can run for an exact time, then shut down and start again later. This enables spacecraft to change orbit in space, and to return to Earth.

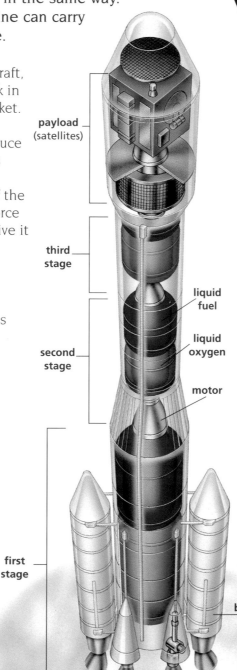

payload (satellites)

third stage

second stage

liquid fuel

liquid oxygen

motor

first stage

booster rocket (solid fuel)

● key words
- firework
- propellant
- satellite
- spacecraft
- stage

GLOSSARY

The glossary gives simple explanations of difficult or specialist words that readers might be unfamiliar with. Words in *italic* have their own glossary entry.

acceleration The rate at which the speed of an object increases.

atom The smallest particle of an *element*. Atoms are made up of a tiny central *nucleus*, surrounded by a cloud of even tinier, fast-moving *electrons*.

condensation The process whereby a gas turns into a liquid.

displacement The amount of a liquid or gas pushed aside (displaced) by a solid object floating on or in it. Displacement is used to measure the volume of large objects like ships.

electromagnetic radiation A kind of radiation that, like light, is made up of *waves*. It travels through a *vacuum* at the speed of light (300,000 kilometres per second).

electron An extremely tiny, fast-moving particle that orbits around the *nucleus* of an *atom*.

element A substance that is made of only one kind of *atom* (as opposed to a compound, which is made up of *molecules* or groups of atoms).

energy That which is needed to make all actions happen. Movement, heat, light, sound and electricity are different forms of energy.

engine A machine that uses *fuel* to create movement.

evaporation The process whereby a liquid turns into gas.

force A push or pull that one object or material exerts on another.

frequency The number of *vibrations* made each second by a *wave,* for example, of sound or light.

friction A *force* that slows a moving object or prevents it from moving.

fuel A material that is burned to produce *energy*. Coal, petrol and gas are all fuels.

gravity The *force* that attracts two objects. Earth's gravity keeps everything on Earth from floating out into space. It makes things flow downhill and fall to the ground.

hydraulic power Power to do work that comes from the pressure of a liquid.

hydroelectric power Electricity that is made using the energy of running water.

lever A rigid bar resting on a fixed point (the fulcrum), which can be turned in order to lift an object or force an object open.

lift The *force* that holds a flying object, such as an aircraft or bird, up in the air.

mass The amount of material (solid, liquid or gas) that something contains.

molecule A group of two or more *atoms* bonded to each other.

nucleus The central part of an *atom,* which contains most of the atom's *mass*.

pneumatic power Power to do work that uses the *pressure* of a gas such as air.

power The rate at which *energy* is turned from one form into another. For example, the power of an engine is the rate at which it can drive a machine.

pressure The amount of *force* with which a liquid or gas pushes on a surface.

relativity A theory developed by the physicist Albert Einstein. His first theory shows that time does not pass at the same speed for someone moving very fast compared with someone who is still. The second theory, general relativity, says that matter, such as stars, makes space curve, causing light rays to bend.

solar power Energy obtained from the Sun, either by storing its heat or by turning its rays into electricity.

theory The reasons that a scientist gives to explain why something happens.

turbine A machine in which blades rotate to produce *power*.

vacuum Complete emptiness; the total absence of air or any other material.

vibration The shaking movement of an object.

wave The way in which sound, light, heat and electricity travel.

weight The *force* with which everything presses down on the ground, water or air beneath it, as a result of *gravity*.

INDEX

Page numbers in **bold** mean that this is where you will find the most information on that subject. If both a heading and a page number are in bold, there is an article with that title. A page number in *italic* means that there is a picture of that subject. There may also be other information about the subject on the same page.

ACKNOWLEDGEMENTS

Key
t = top; c = centre; b = bottom; r = right; l = left;
back = background; fore = foreground

Artwork
Baker, Julian: 18 b. **D'Achille, Gino:** 4 t; 7 tr; 18 cl; 21 tr; 41 tr. **Franklin, Mark:** 10 t; 15 tl, tr; 19 b; 22 br; 24 bc; 27 cr; 29 tr; 34 tr; 36 bl; 39 b; 40 cr; 41 bl; 43 t; 45 c. **Hadler, Terry:** 9 tl. **Learoyd, Tracey:** 32 bl. **Oxford Designers and Illustrators:** 13 cr; 19 cl; 42 bl; 44 c. **Saunders, Michael:** 16 tr; 17 t; 19 tl; 21 b; 25 b; 30 b; 33 t; 38 cr. **Sneddon, James:** 28 cl. **Visscher, Peter:** 4 tl; 5 main; 6 tr; 7 tl; 9 b; 11 tl; 13 tl; 14 tl; 16 tl; 18 tl; 21 tl; 23 tl; 24 tl; 25 tl; 26 tl, cr; 28 tl; 29 tl; 30 tl; 31 tl; 32 tl; 34 tl; 36 tl; 38 tl; 40 tl; 41 tl; 42 tl; 44 tl; 45 tl. **Woods, Michael:** 20 t.

Photos
The publishers would like to thank the following for permission to use their photographs.

Allsport: 4 b (Jon Ferrey); 9 tr (Clive Mason); 11 r (F. Rickard Vandysadt); 13 b (Zoom); 29 bl (Brian Bahr).

BAE Systems: 44 tr.

Corbis: 7 b (Tony Arruza); 10 br (Adam Woolfitt); 12 bl (Vince Streano); 18 tr (Richard T. Novitz); 28 bl; 32 tr (Sally A. Morgan); 36 tr (Hubert Stadler); 37 bl (Phil Schermeister); 43 b.

David Mellor: 14 tr (Pete Hill).

Digital Vision: 6 b; 35 br; 35 cl; 35 tr; 38–39 t; 40 bl.

H. J. Banks & Co Ltd.: 16 cl.

Haddon Davies: 8 t; 12; 14 bl, br; 16 br; 22 tl, tr; 23 bl.

Michel Brigaud: 37 tr.

NASA: 23 tr.

Oxford Scientific Films: 17 b (Gerard Soury); 27 t (Mark Jones).

Photodisc: 19 tr; 22 bl.

Science and Society Picture Library: 41 c.

Science Photo Library: 8 b; 20 bl (Dale Boyer/NASA); 24 tr (Sheila Terry); 25 tr; 26 cl (Doug Allan); 27 br (Dr Arthur Tucker); 30 r (Andrew Syred); 31 br (Tony Craddock); 38 bl (Peter Menzel); 42 tr (Astrid & Hanns-Frieder Michler); 45 tr (Françoise Sauze).

Volkswagen: 15 br.